A Simple Series
# CHRISTMAS
Presents

# TELL THE WORLD JESUS IS BORN!

**AVAILABLE PRODUCTS:**

**PHYSICAL PRODUCTS**

| | |
|---|---|
| Choral Book | 45757-2927-7 |
| CD Preview Pak | 45757-2927-1 |
| Listening CD | 45757-2927-2 |
| Split-Track Accompaniment CD | 45757-2927-3 |
| Split-Track Accompaniment DVD | 45757-2927-6 |
| Soprano/Alto Rehearsal Track CD | 45757-2927-0 |
| Tenor/Bass Rehearsal Track CD | 45757-2927-5 |

A 25-MINUTE
MINI-MUSICAL
ARRANGED ESPECIALLY
FOR UNISON AND
TWO-PART CHOIRS

CREATED BY
SUE C. SMITH AND
MASON BROWN

 a division of

www.brentwoodbenson.com
© MMXV Brentwood-Benson Music Publications,
101 Winners Circle, Brentwood, TN 37027
All Rights Reserved. Unauthorized Duplication Prohibited.

# Contents

Joy to the World! —————————————————————————3

The Christmas Song ——————————————————————9

A Nativity Medley ———————————————————————19
    For Unto Us a Child Is Born /
    Away in a Manger / Silent Night

O Little Town of Bethlehem ———————————————————28

Come, Let Us Worship Medley —————————————————30
    O Come, All Ye Faithful
    *with* Here I Am to Worship

Go, Tell It on the Mountain ——————————————————39
    *with* Mighty to Save

# The Christmas Song

Words and Music by
RONNIE FREEMAN and SUE C. SMITH
*Arranged by Bradley Knight*

**NARRATOR:** *(Music starts)* "Sing for joy, and let it be heard all over the world today! Jesus is born, salvation is here, and we have every reason to celebrate. This long-awaited good news was given first to a simple Jewish girl, then to a poor carpenter. At last, on the night of His birth, a host of angels proclaimed it to lowly shepherds. "Fear not! For unto you is born this day a Savior, who is Christ the Lord!"

© Copyright 2010 Universal Music – Brentwood Benson Publishing / CCTB Music / New Spring Publishing / Lehajoes Music (ASCAP) (Administered at CapitolCMGPublishing.com). All rights reserved. Used by permission.
**PLEASE NOTE: Copying of this music is NOT covered by the CCLI license. For CCLI information call 1-800-234-2446.**

# A Nativity Medley
## *For Unto Us a Child Is Born / Away in a Manger / Silent Night*

*Arranged by Bradley Knight*

**NARRATOR:** *(Music starts)* This story was prophesied long before it happened in the writings of Isaiah: "The people walking in darkness have seen a great light; on those living in the land of deep darkness a light has dawned… For to us a child is born, to us a son is given, and the government will be on his shoulders. And he will be called Wonderful Counselor, Mighty God, Everlasting Father, Prince of Peace…"

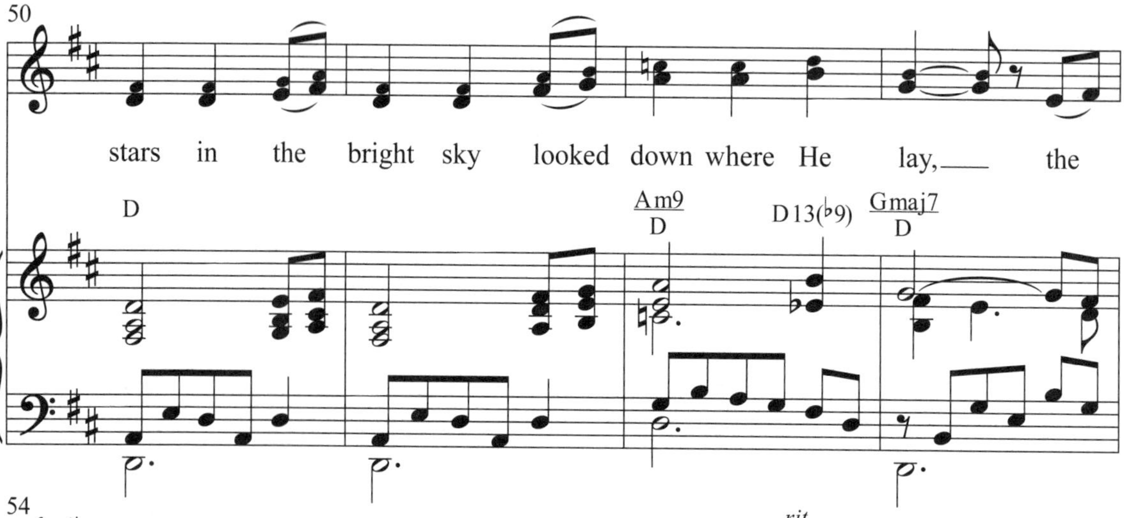
50
stars in the bright sky looked down where He lay, the
D
Am9/D
D13(♭9)
Gmaj7/D

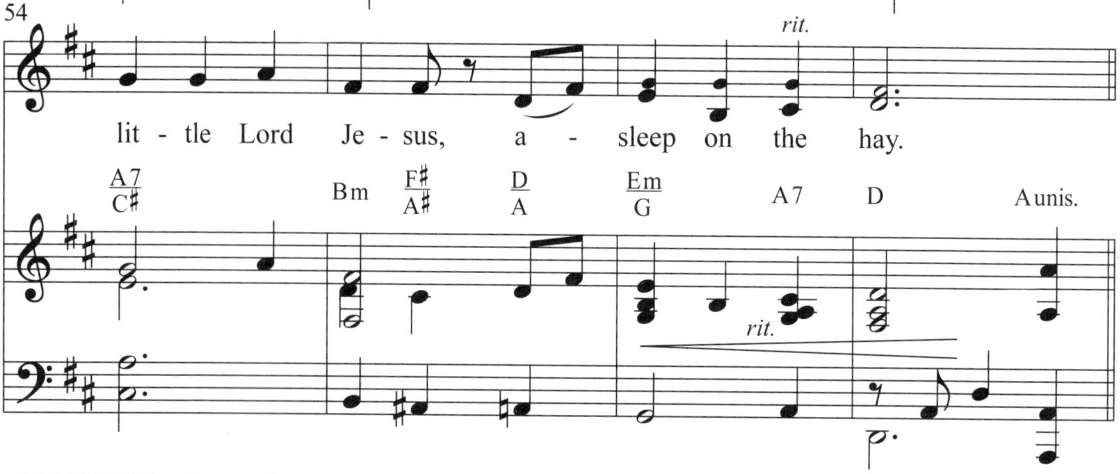
54
rit.
lit - tle Lord Je - sus, a - sleep on the hay.
A7/C♯
Bm
F♯/A♯
D/A
Em/G
A7
D
A unis.
rit.

NARRATOR: From the greatest oratorios to the simplest songs sung by children, this glorious news that God so loved the world and sent His only begotten Son has changed hearts and lives wherever it has been told. Every Christmas, the old familiar carols remind us once again of the incredible Gift we were given on that night in Bethlehem when Mary brought forth her firstborn son and laid Him in a manger. And so we sing once more…

22
D
58
a tempo
Am/D
D7(♭9)
Gmaj7/D

62
A7/C♯
A♯°7
Bm
Am7/C

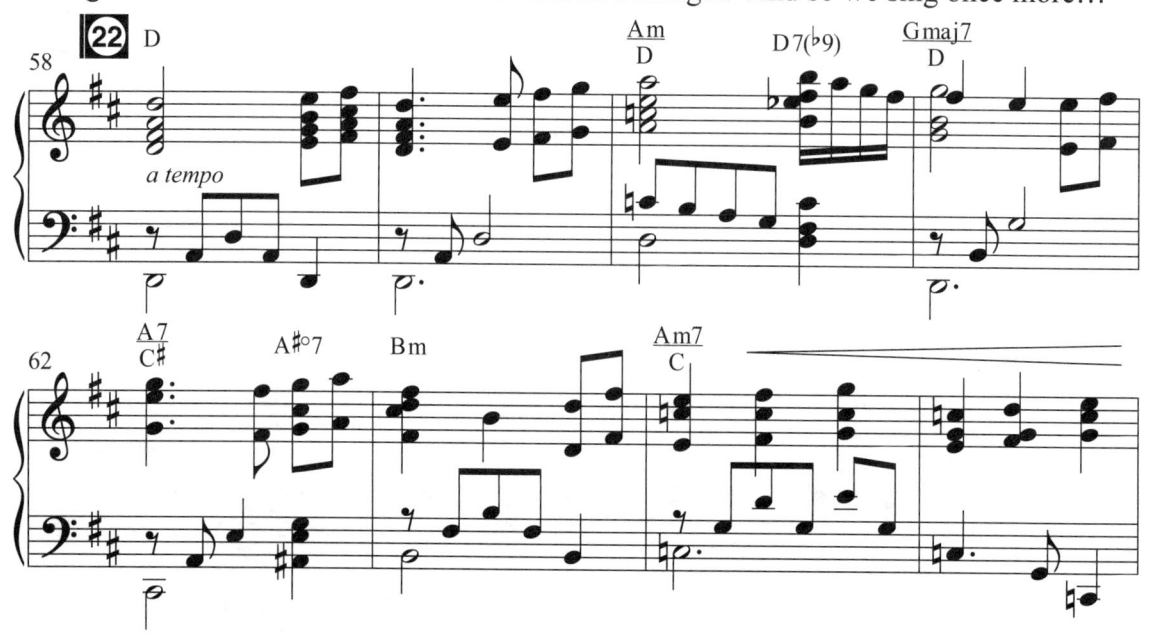

# Come, Let Us Worship Medley
## O Come, All Ye Faithful *with* Here I Am to Worship

*Arranged by Russell Mauldin*

**NARRATOR:** Come to the manger with joy and with hope today. *(Music starts)* Come with a song of thanksgiving and a shout of victory. God has kept His promise. His Son has come to give His life a ransom for many, to bear our cross and defeat death with His resurrection. This is the Gospel of Jesus Christ!

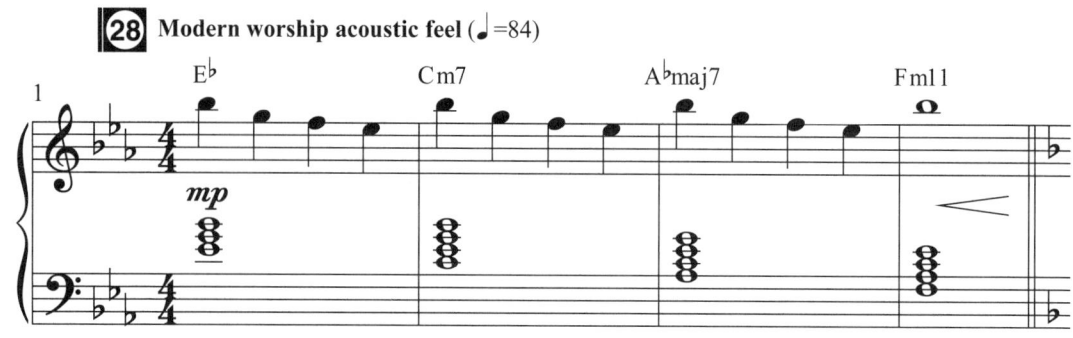

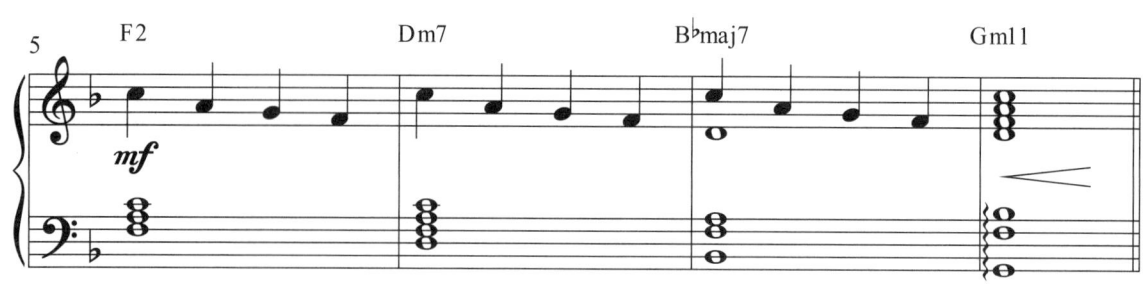

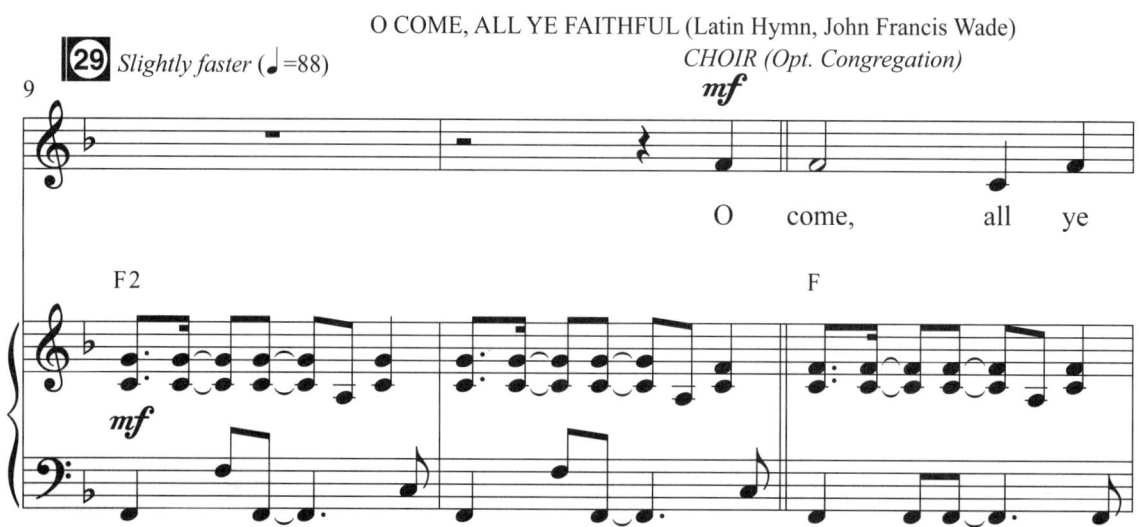

Arr. © Copyright 2013 Universal Music - Brentwood Benson Publishing (ASCAP)
(Administered at CapitolCMGPublishing.com). All rights reserved. Used by permission.
**PLEASE NOTE:** Copying of this music is NOT covered by the CCLI license. For CCLI information call 1-800-234-2446.

won-der-ful to me. So, here I am to wor-ship! Here I am to wor-ship!

*rit.* *Slightly broader* ($\quarter=79$)

We give You all the glo-ry! We give You all the glo-ry! We give You all the

38

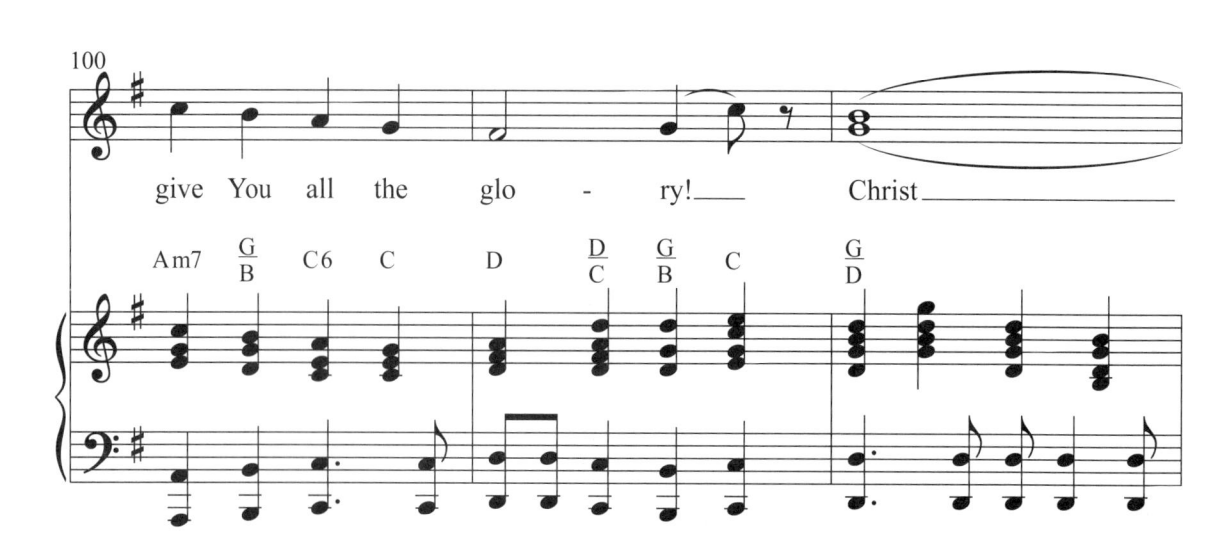

glo - ry! Christ the Lord! We give You all the glo - ry! Christ the Lord!

# Go, Tell It on the Mountain
## with Mighty to Save

Lyrics by
JOHN W. WORK, JR.

Traditional Spiritual
New Lyrics by SUE C. SMITH,
DAVID MOFFITT and TRAVIS COTTRELL
Arranged by Travis Cottrell

**NARRATOR:** *(Music starts)* What are we to do with this good news of His birth? Like the shepherds, we fall in worship before Him. Like the wise men, we bring what is most precious to us, even our very lives, and lay them down in surrender. And then, we go out to make this news known to everyone. It's Christmas, and Jesus has come!"

© Copyright 2014 Universal Music - Brentwood Benson Publishing / Great Revelation Music / TimeChange Music (ASCAP) / Universal Music - Brentwood Benson Songs / Songs from Bobb Avenue (BMI) (Administered at CapitolCMGPublishing.com). All rights reserved. Used by permission.
**PLEASE NOTE:** Copying of this music is NOT covered by the CCLI license. For CCLI information call 1-800-234-2446.

**40** *CHOIR*

Go, tell it on the mountain, over the hills and ev-'ry-where. Go, tell it on the mountain that Jesus Christ is born!

Go, tell about the

shep- herds, the star up in the sky, the an- gels shout- ing glo- ry, our hope is burn- ing bright! Go, tell it on the moun- tain, o- ver the hills and ev-'ry- where.

Go, tell it on the mountain that Jesus Christ is born! Go tell how mercy found you, how love has made you new. Go tell the weak and wea - ry how grace has brought you through.

Go, tell it on the moun - tain, o - ver the hills and ev - 'ry - where. Go, tell it on the moun - tain that Je - sus Christ is born!

44

*Je-sus is born!*

MIGHTY TO SAVE (Reuben Morgan, Ben Fielding)

*Shine your light and let the whole world sing_____ for the glo - ry*

© Copyright 2006 Hillsong Music Publishing (APRA)
(Administered in the US and Canada at CapitolCMGPublishing.com). All rights reserved. Used by permission.

**[48]**

of the ris - en King.

*(MEN sing cue notes)*

Shine your light and let the whole world sing

for the glo - ry of the ris - en

**[49]**

King. Go, sing of your sal -

-vation, the joy that nev-er ends. Go, *building* tell the world that Je-sus will one day come a-gain! Go, tell it on the moun-tain, o-ver the hills and ev-'ry-where.

47

Go, tell it on the moun-tain\_ that Je-sus Christ is born! Go, tell it on the moun-tain, o-ver the hills and ev-'ry-where.\_ Go, tell it on the moun-tain\_ that Je-sus Christ is born!\_

110
Je-sus is born!
Dm7 Csus
F/A Bb2
Dm7 Csus
113
F/A Bb2
Dm7 Csus
F/A Bb2
116
Je - sus is born!
Dm7 Csus
F(no3)
53
120
F Bb2
mf
Dm7 Csus
F Bb2

**123** *MEN* *mf*

Tell the world, tell the world

Dm7    Csus      F    B♭2

**125**

that He is born! Jesus is born!

Dm7    Csus      F    B♭2

**127** *ALL* *(MEN sing cue notes)* *mf*

Tell the world, tell the world

Dm7    Csus      F/A    B♭2

**129**

that He is born, Jesus is born!

Dm7    Csus      F/A    B♭2

Tell the world, tell the world that He is born, Jesus is born! Go, tell it on the mountain, over the hills and ev'rywhere. Go, tell it on the mountain that

Je - sus Christ is born!

Je - sus is born!

*(MEN sing cue notes)*
Tell the world, tell the world that He is born!

*molto rit.*
Je - sus is born!

Celebrate the reason for the season
with these Best-Selling Christmas Musicals from the

# READY TO SING SERIES –
## America's #1 Selling Church Choir Series

Arranged by RUSSELL MAULDIN

These musicals are perfect for the small to medium-sized choir, or the large choir with limited rehearsal time. Available in Easy SATB.

# ORDER YOUR PREVIEW PAK TODAY!

**The Ready To Sing Series** available –
Exclusively through the **Brentwood Choral Club!**

Call **1-800-846-7664**, visit **www.brentwoodbenson.com**
or order from your local Christian retailer today!